Sh*t My Boss Says

By

Bianca Ku

Shit My Boss Says
Copyright © 2014 by Bianca Ku
All rights reserved
ISBN-13:978-1496016997
ISBN-10:1496016998
www.fartdiary.net

The author appreciates your respect of the copyright on this work. This Book is for your personal use only. The author has done her best to verify facts and credit resources used. In the unfortunate event that any material is incorrect or has been used without proper permission, please contact us immediately so that this oversight can be corrected.

No part of this publication may be reproduced or transmitted in any form (electronic, mechanical or otherwise) without the express written consent of the author. Kindly support the author's efforts by introducing this work to others.

Join Newsletter list

To join Bianca Ku's Newsletter and be notified about FREE book promos and when new books are released by the author.

Click here to join Bianca Ku's Newsletter list

For more books by this author, visit

Amazon's Bianca Ku's Page

Books

Sh*t My Boss Says
Turkey Farts
Dog Farts
Santa Farts
Fart Diary
Dinosaur Farts

"Look at yourself, Johnson-- your desk is a mess, you're behind on your work and your attitude stinks. I'm starting to think you don't appreciate the $4 an hour we're paying you."

"I laid the entire staff off. How do you feel about a 140-hour work week?"

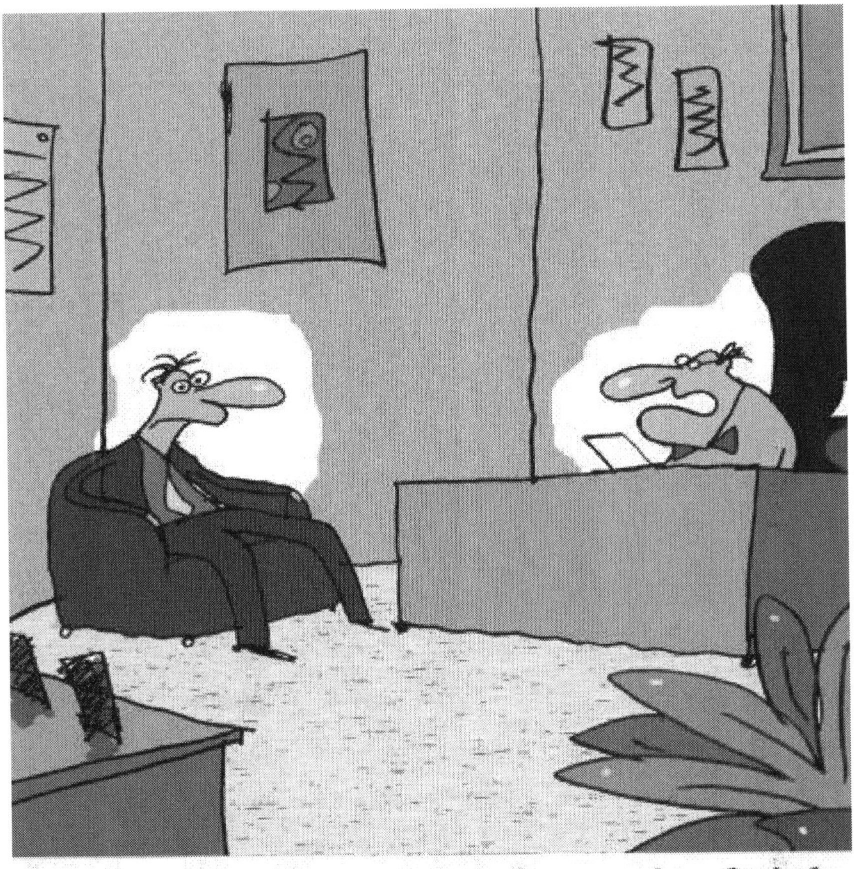

"Relax, Mr. Gray, this is just a simple job interview for a sales position. So, please stop pleading the 5th everytime I ask you a question."

"The boss said you can come back in now. But never, ever make eye contact with him again."

"Go up to accounting and pick up the Randel file. You may want to take this. Those guys don't fool around."

"I've got to let you go, Johnson. But in honor of your service, I'm allowing you to keep your email address."

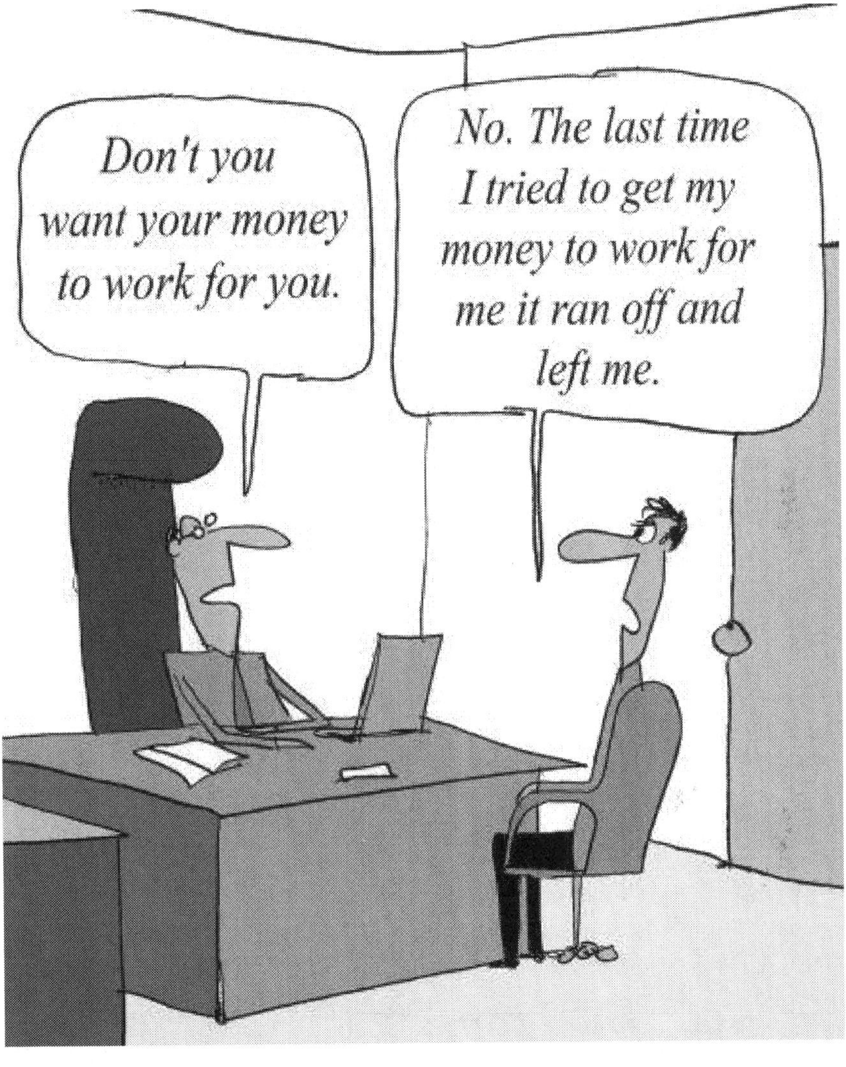
Don't you want your money to work for you.
No. The last time I tried to get my money to work for me it ran off and left me.

"Accounting has calculated how much we've paid you compared to how much work you've done. You owe the company $53,972."

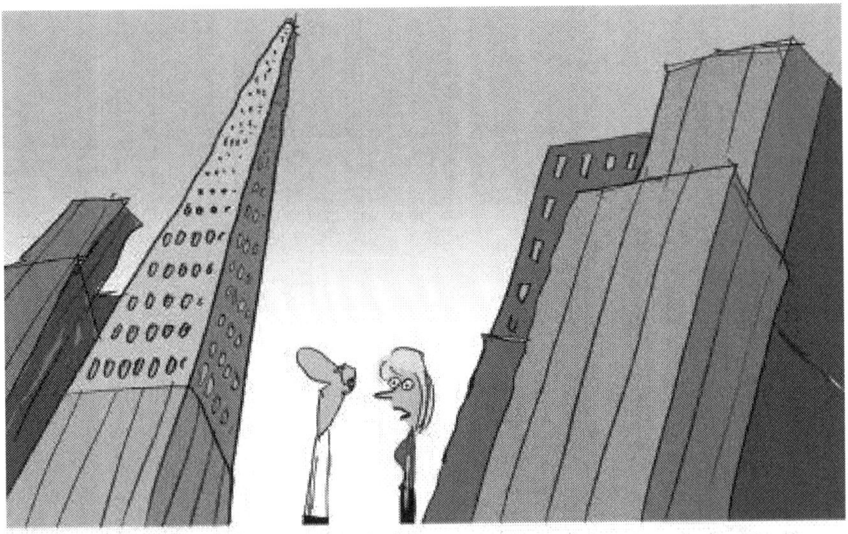

"I work on the 187th floor. I hate my job, but the walk up has done wonders for my figure."

"You should consider yourself lucky. Some of the employees don't have any company vehicle."

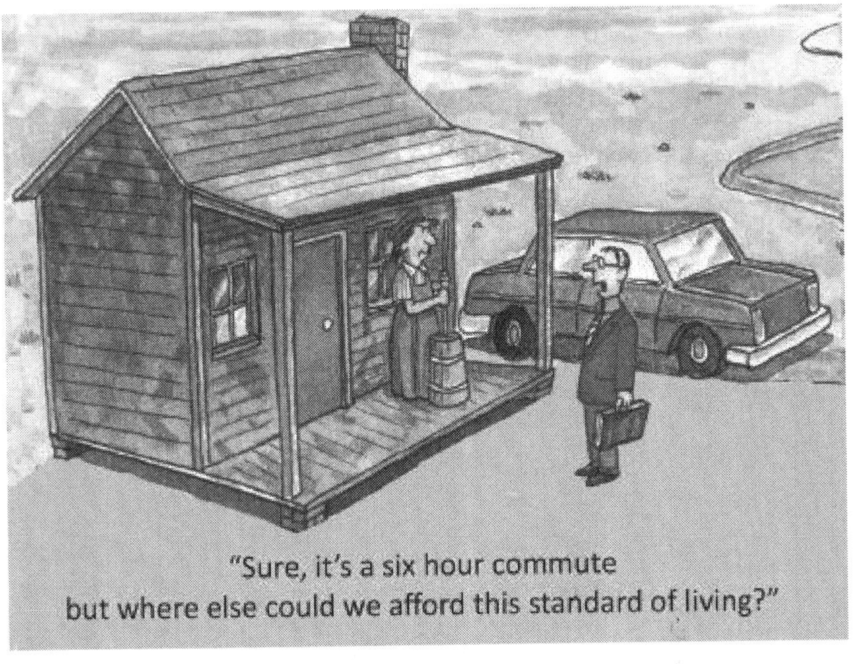

"Sure, it's a six hour commute
but where else could we afford this standard of living?"

"I DON'T THINK WE'RE IN THE CARIBBEAN. I THINK I'LL ASK SANTA FOR A NEW NAVIGATIONAL SYSTEM."

"We were going to hire you, but a background check showed you pulled a girl's ponytail in the 2nd grade. We don't need abusive people working here."

"I'm your best friend, not your employee. I don't need an appointment to see you."

"Do you think my book on ants will start a bidding war?"

"After extensive X-rays and blood tests, we've confirmed what we already suspected-- you're not big-boned, you're fat."

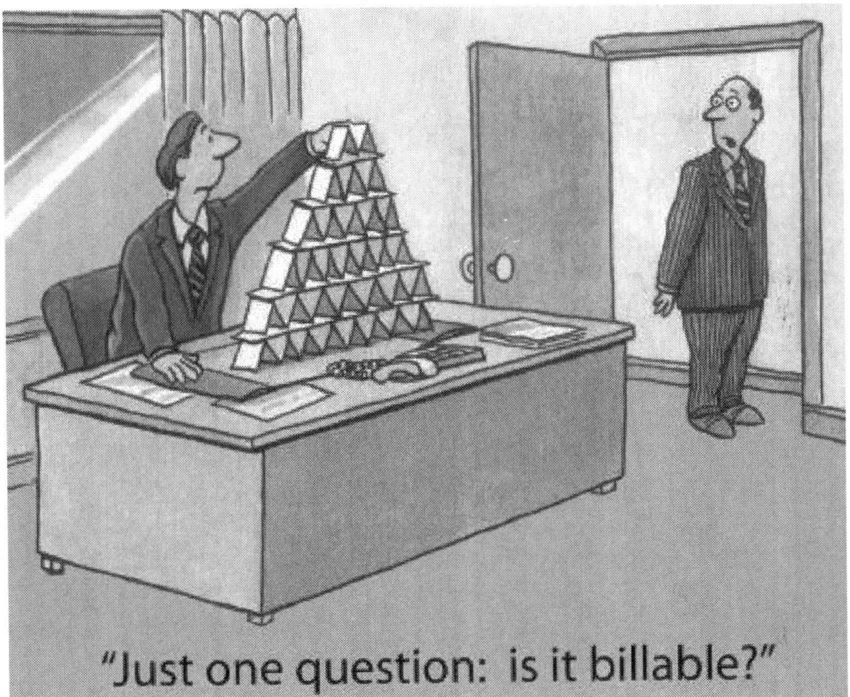

"Just one question: is it billable?"

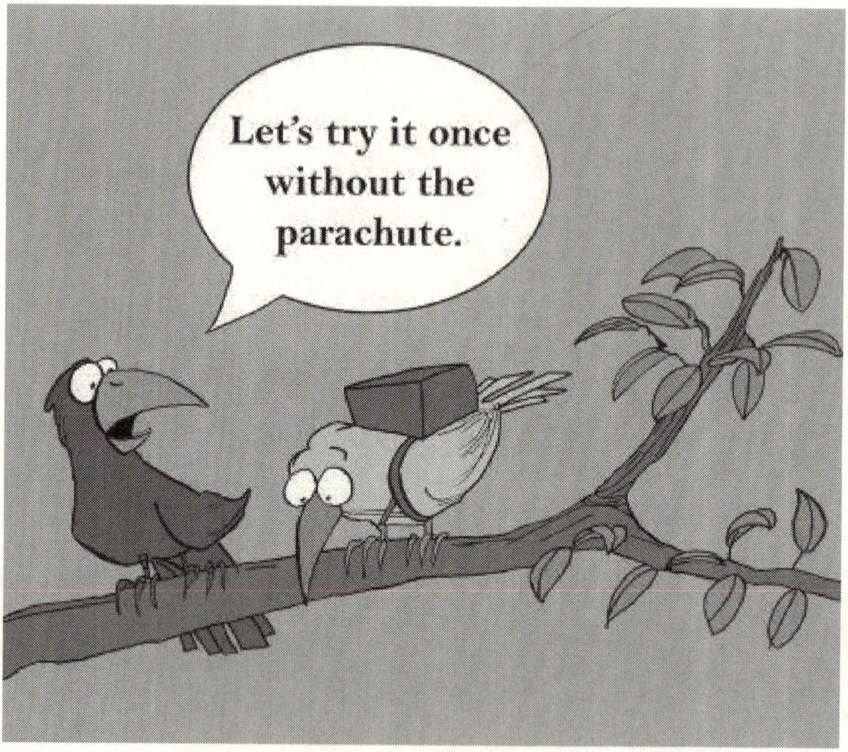
Let's try it once without the parachute.

The joke about 'milking' hung in the air like a bloated udder.

"I just sold enough blood to keep my website afloat for another month. Now, if you excuse me, I need to go pass out."

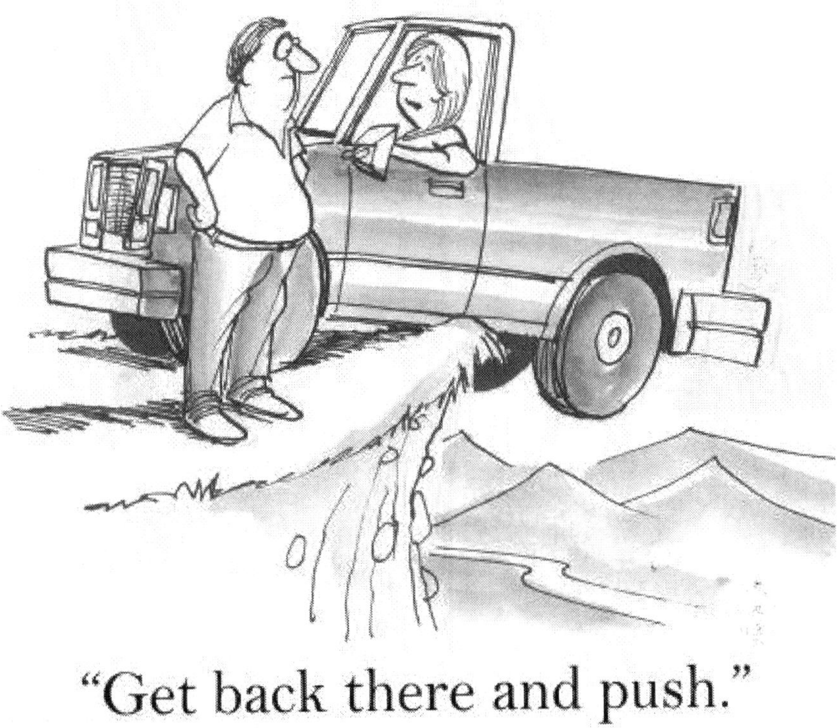

"Get back there and push."

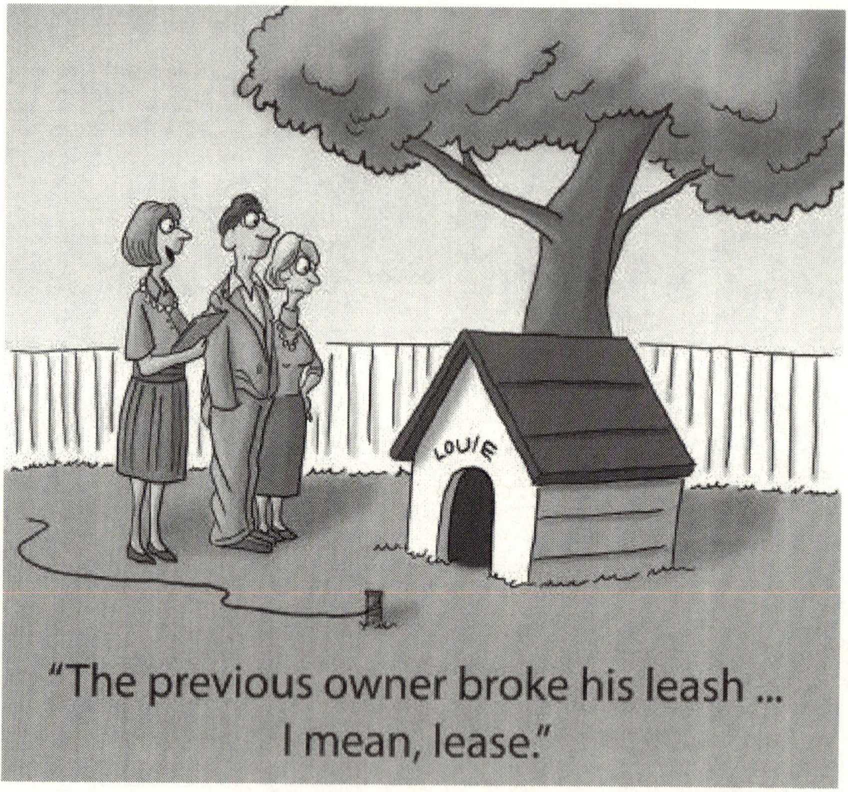
LOUIE

"The previous owner broke his leash ...
I mean, lease."

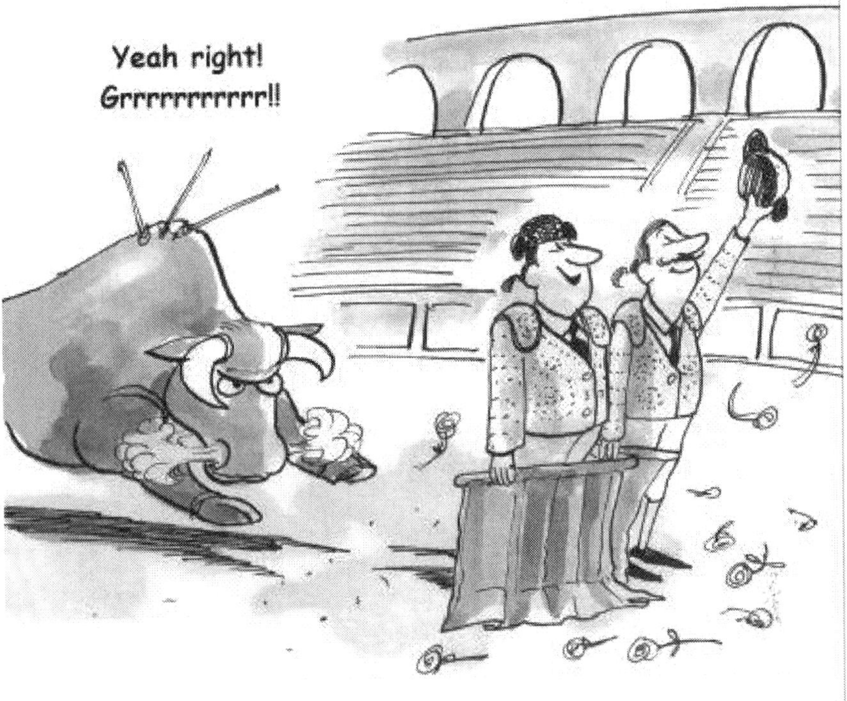
Yeah right!
Grrrrrrrrrrr!!

"Ok, we finished that one off.
Let's move on to the next one."

"You busy?"

"How does my morning look?"

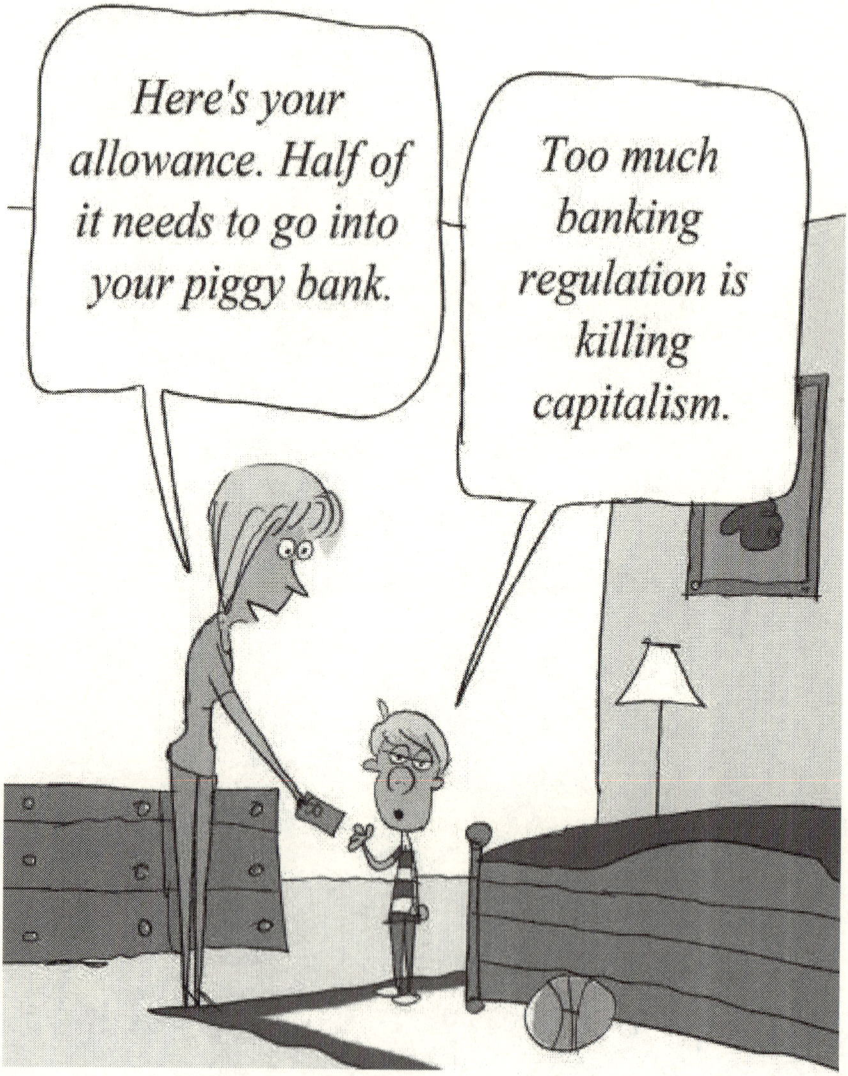
Here's your allowance. Half of it needs to go into your piggy bank.
Too much banking regulation is killing capitalism.

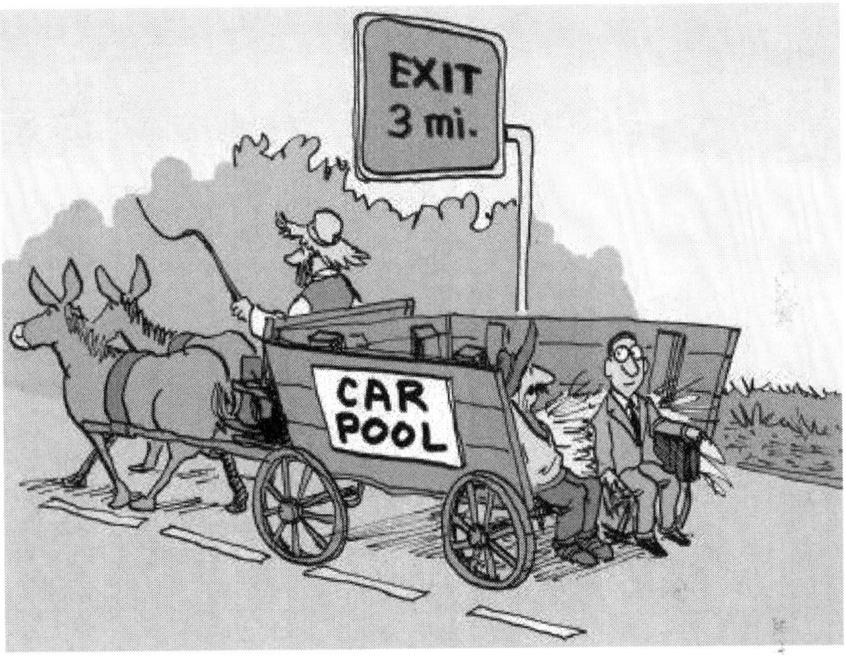
EXIT
3 mi.
CAR
POOL

"Dude, touring with a punk rock band was fun, but what I'd really like to do is be CEO of a Fortune 500 company."

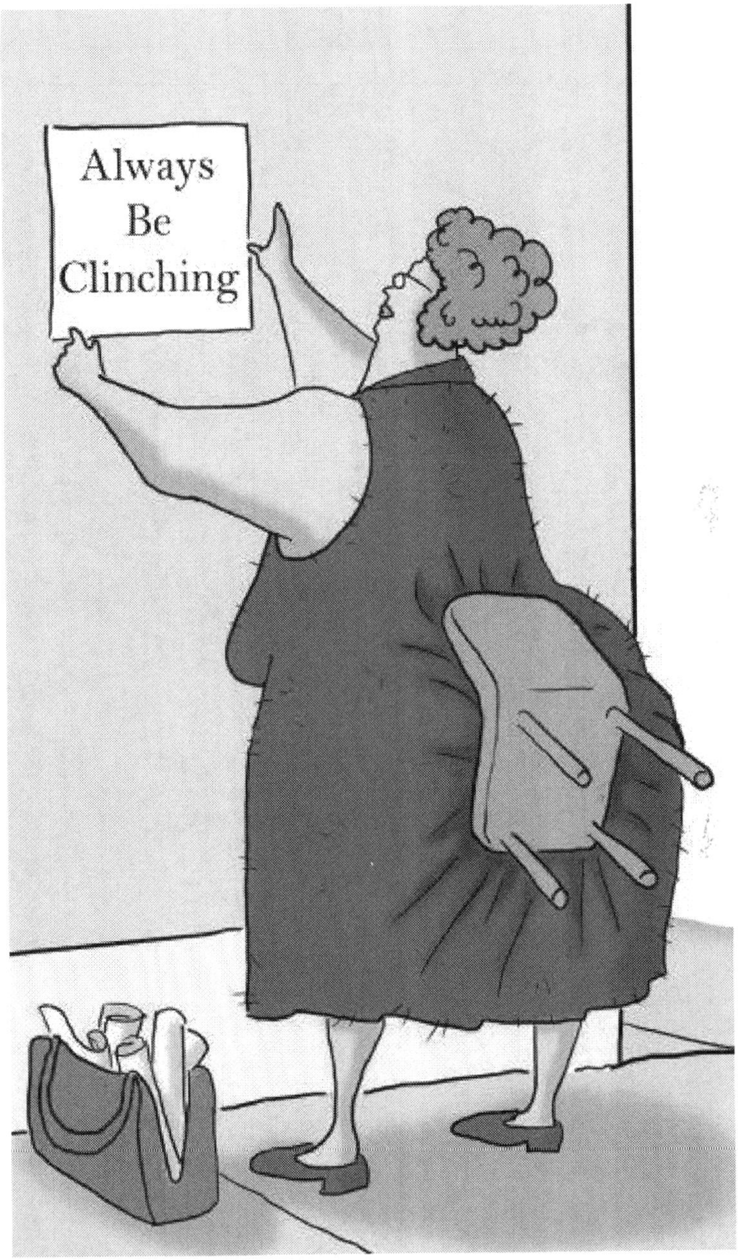
Always
Be
Clinching

"Your mother wants a parade,
so rip up some paper into confetti."

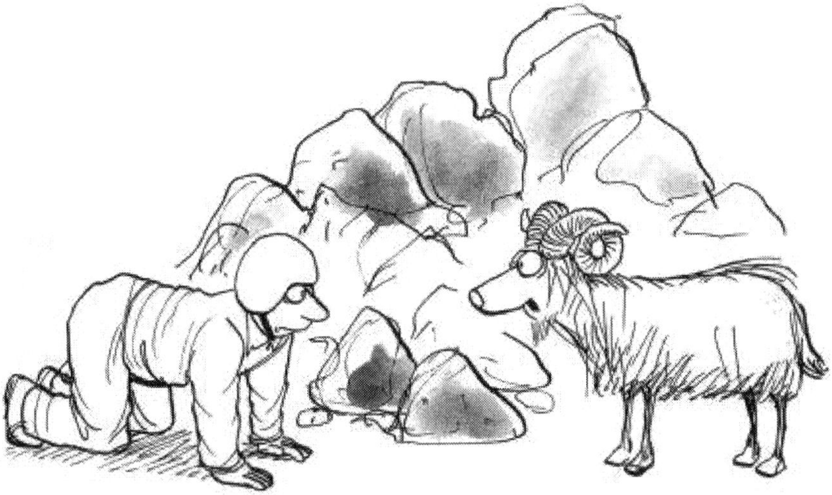

"Ready for your first lesson in conflict resolution?"

"Copy machine's down again."

"Everything cool is to be found in the deep woods."

"Want my pickle?"

"I'm looking for an eight minute mile pace. Ready, and ..."

"*Apparently you're not the only one who needs to start exercising.*"

"I know you three wanted the promotion to V.P. However, my dog has been a loyal friend, so he gets the job."

His face exuded calm, but his tail betrayed him.

"*How sweet, he's smiling. He must be dreaming about me.*"

"Go easy on me. I just had my annual review."

"Yes, Mr. James is in. What excuse would you like to hear for him not seeing you?"

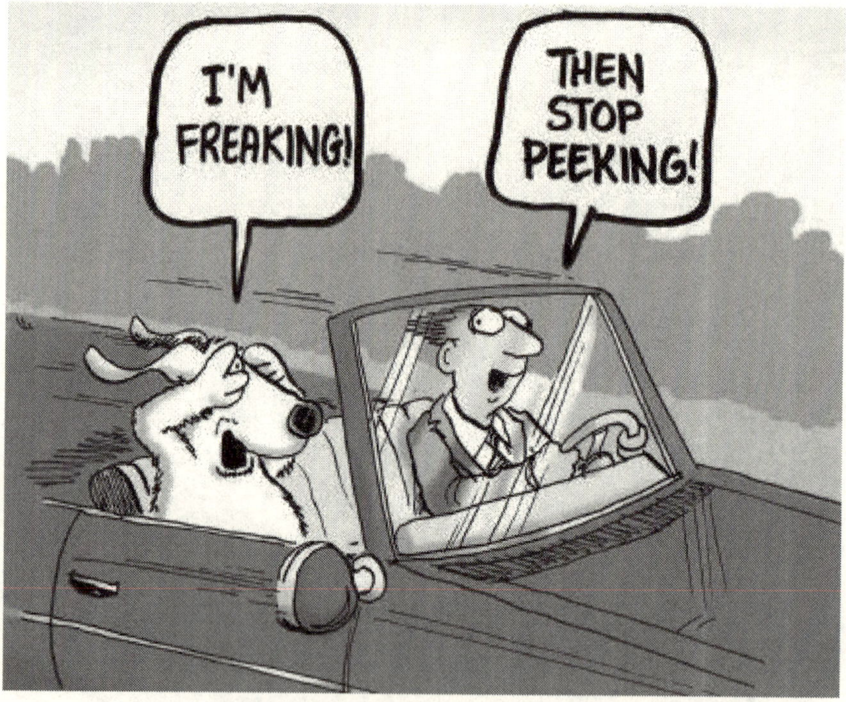
I'M FREAKING!
THEN STOP PEEKING!

"Who threw that fur ball?!"

"The gatorade is his."

"I made a list of all the mistakes in your golf swing. I hope you have some extra time, because this may take awhile."

"Let me know if I am distracting you."

"I'm afraid he's becoming too dependent on technology. I don't think he could find his rear end without a GPS."

"And here we have the half bathroom."

"It's important to note we really did try hard."

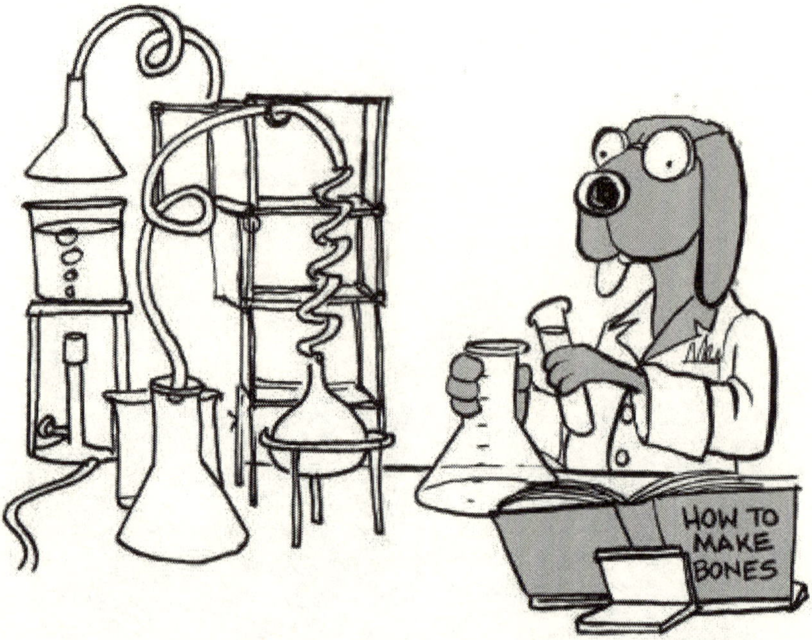
HOW TO
MAKE
BONES

"At least the hula-hoop still fits."

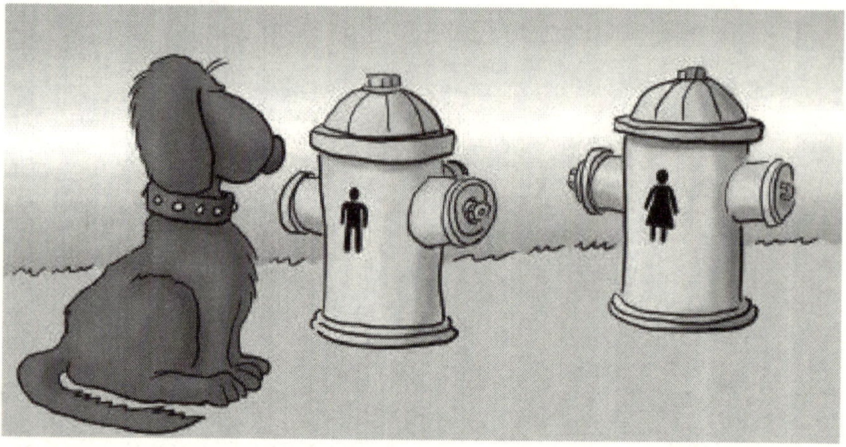

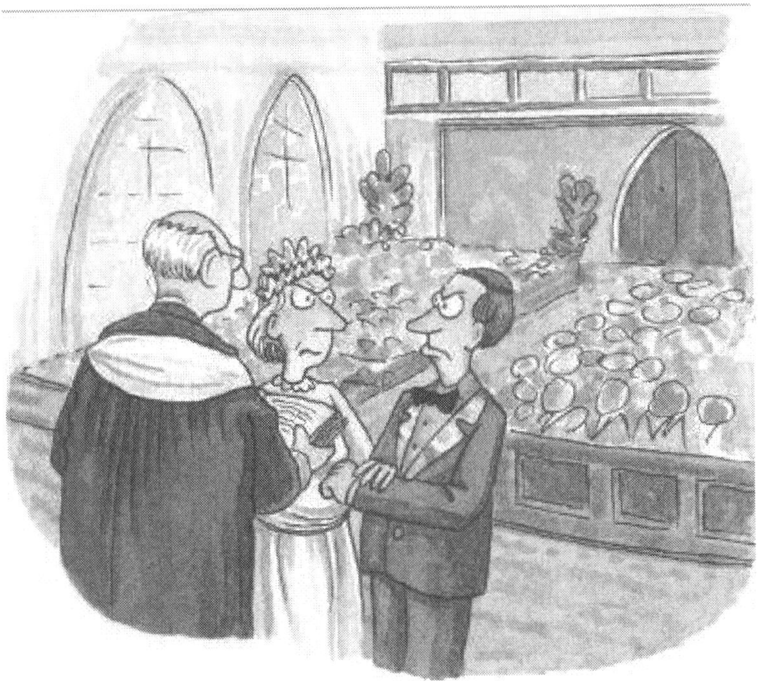

"I'd appreciate it if you wouldn't cry 'I want my mommy' every time you don't close a deal"

"What kind of immortality plan do you offer?"

"I tried to warn you against inflatable furniture."

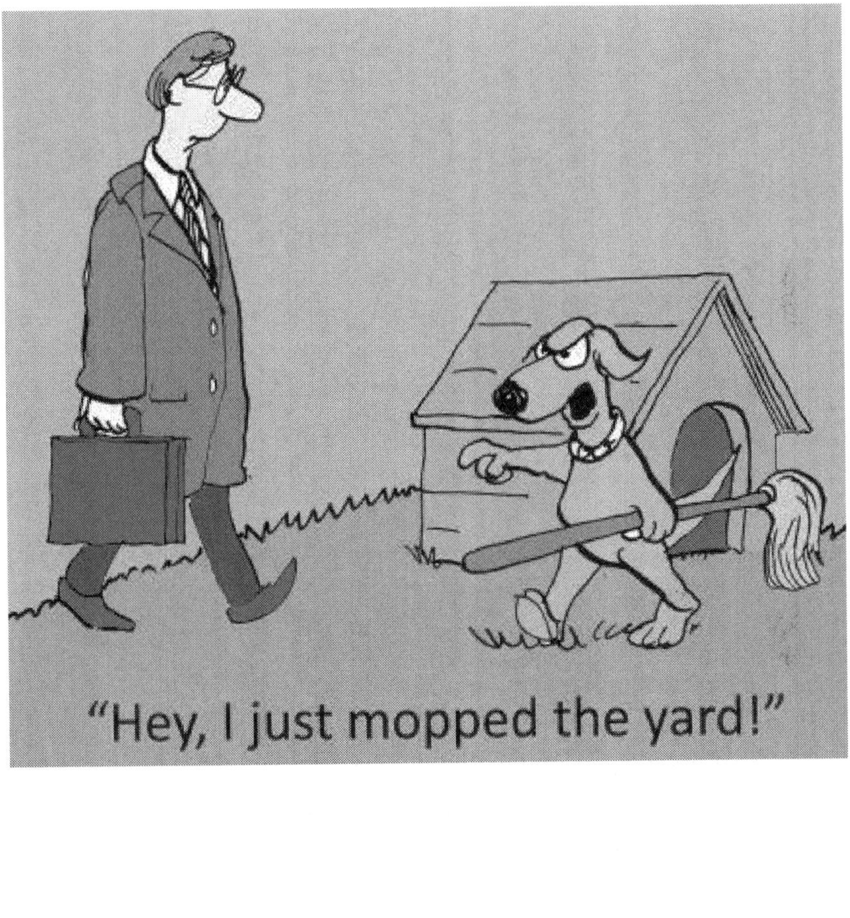

"Hey, I just mopped the yard!"

NOT BAD. TWENTY MINUTES AND THIRTEEN SECONDS BEFORE HE SAID SOMETHING STUPID.

"Dad, I've decided to get my personal injury lawyer involved."

"Not only can I not find the middle class tax cut, I can't find the middle class."

"And when I get home, there better be some fresh milk for my cereal."

"I'll get right to the point, Johnson--we're not happy with your job performance over the last 10 years. We want our money back."

That wasn't barking!
That was me giving a motivational speech!

"Isn't that like my Henry to spend all day raking the leaves!"

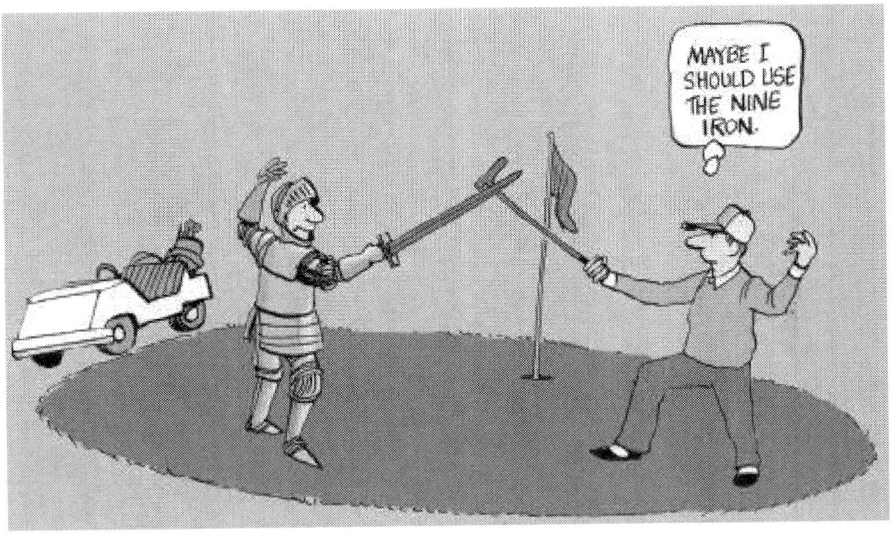
MAYBE I SHOULD USE THE NINE IRON.

"I was King of the Jungle,
but then I went into non-profit."

"I've been in this business a long time and I'm telling you, that is not laughing."

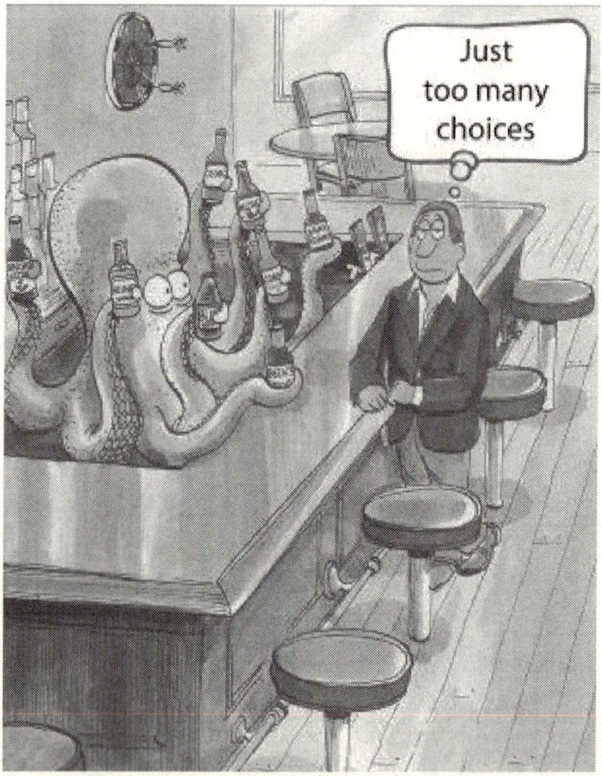
Just
too many
choices

"I'm moving you into this office because it overlooks the unemployment office. I thought you could use the motivation."

"I may transfer you out of Acquisitions."

"The good news is we are sending you overseas."

"Mr. Kennings was going to interview you for the job, until he heard you actually wanted to get paid."

"First you wanted a lamp, now you want a desk. You're becoming a real pain in the neck."

"I just want to say for the record that sumo wrestling is a rotten way to choose top pet."

"Please don't ask me to remind you to do anything else for awhile."

"Our company finally turned a profit, so the church sent a priest to witness the miracle."

"Mr. Billings realizes you traveled a long way to meet with him. However, he decided to change the meeting until next week."

"Before copiers we used to have to drop our pants and have co-workers draw our rear ends manually."

"My profile says 'In a relationship', but his says 'It's complicated'."

"I have really gotten into this Roman History course."

"I certainly didn't mean to tear your nice new safari shirt."

"I've learned how much self-discipline I have. I've played 358 rounds of golf in the 2 weeks I've been self-employed."

"Be forewarned...Mr. Jenkins likes to keep his employees on a short leash."

"We're members of the shrinking middle class."

"My skills travel well."

"Sure it's a smart phone. It has computing capabilities."

He waited patiently,
but his chips refused to fall.

"My son here is failing out of medical school. So to earn extra credit, he'll be operating on you."

"If my weasel of a husband files as head of household, it's tax fraud."

"Who says the government doesn't have a sense of humor. After convicting you of not filing your taxes, they made your inmate number the same as your tax idenification number."

"You're far too clever to just fire."

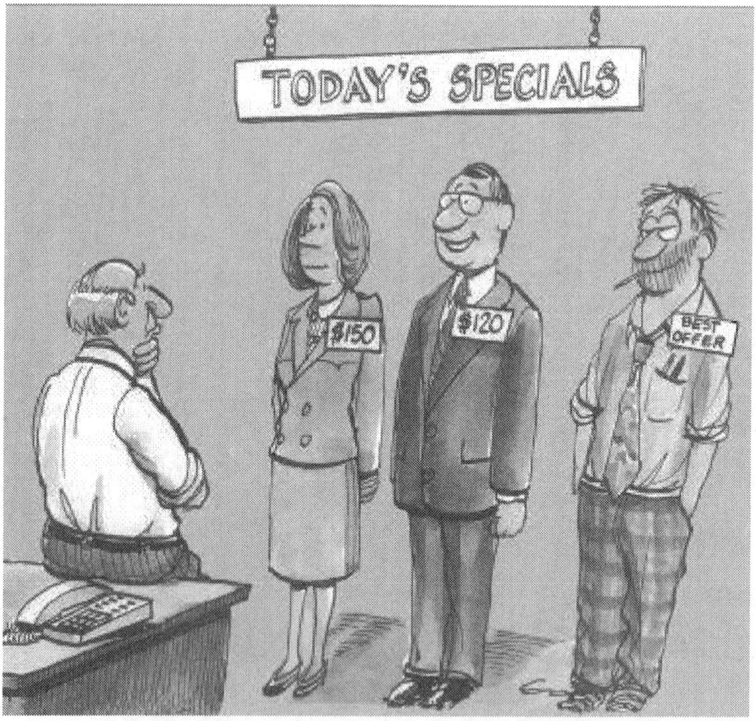
TODAY'S SPECIALS
$150
$120
BEST OFFER

"Our company needs a tougher image. So from here on out we'll answer the phone with the greeting, 'what the hell do you want?!'"

"Are you certain you tried hard enough to get to the meeting on time?"

"We think you have an unhealthy obsession with upgrading your computer. You're to check into rehab on Monday."

"We may have gained weight."

"Tell my wife I can't speak to her right now. However, she can send me a fax detailing the info on whether she had a boy or a girl."

"Halfway through the divorce I found out my husband is a wizard."

"If I have to be at these boring meetings,
I might as well get something out of it."

"I'm a little concerned, Randolph. Six of our top competitors have written to thank us for hiring you."

"I'm concerned that you don't give a sniff."

"Due to corporate cutbacks, we're all going to have to sacrifice. Which is why I'm only playing nine holes today, instead of my customary 18."

"You've spent the last 20 years in college. What made you stop hiding from the real world?"

"There's not enough blame to go around.
There's only enough for you."

"The employees are rioting and burning their desks. Cutting their pay after buying yourself a new corporate jet wasn't such a hot idea after all."

"That company credit card was for business purposes only. So, would you kindly return that Harley Davidson you bought?"

"I'm meeting my boss here in about a half hour. Three more of these and I just might be able to tolerate him."

"Currently, my assets are diversified. They're split up among my 4 ex-wives."

"My doctor said it would relieve stress if I did something really, really fun. Peterson, you're fired."

"I started freelancing because I didn't like working for other people. Of course, they didn't like me working for them either."

"I've set as this year's goal to get out of my parents' basement and into their garage apartment."

"Before I get into why I called you in here, let me first say that you're just the type of go-getter who won't be unemployed long."

"His name is Thomas 3-iron Smythe. My husband is a golfer."

"What's with the truck? Just how much golf equipment did you buy?"

"I assume all this playing will lead to innovation."

"My intern has worked out wonderfully.
You really should consider getting one."

"Thanks for the 'Good luck on your new job search' card. But I wasn't aware I was looking for a new job."

"Helen, you're the team leader, why don't you jump first?"

"You better believe that a critique of this lousy date is going up on Facebook!"

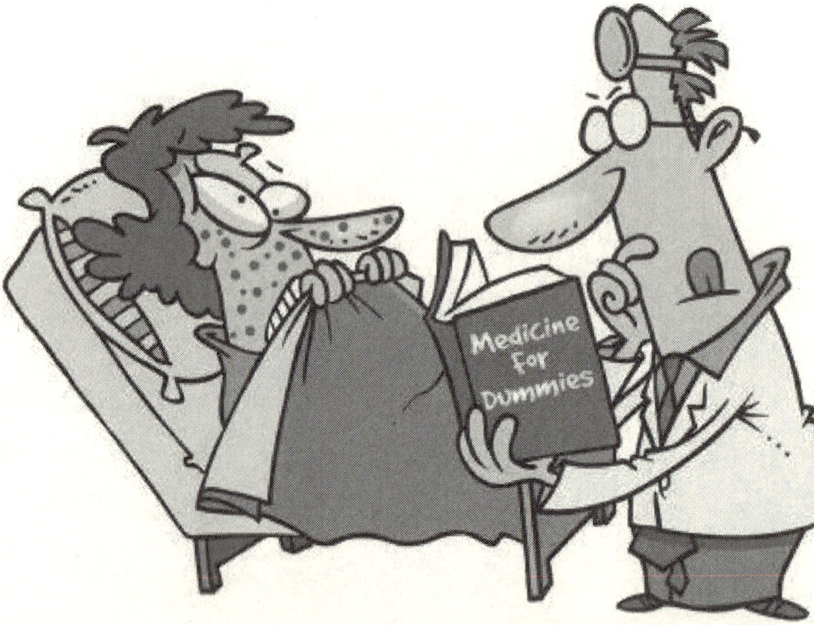
Medicine for Dummies

YOU KNOW, IF YOU CAN WAIT THREE WEEKS, COLD MEDICINE WILL BE ON SALE.
COLD MEDICINE

"If you'd like to know if you got the job or not, go to www.NotinaMillionYears.com, where the answer is posted."

"Fredericks, you're lazy, greedy and out of touch with your fellow employees. Welcome to management."

"Actually, we're not hiring. We hold lots of interviews like this one, so our competition thinks we're busy."

"Go up and tell Jennings that though I appreciate his frustration, he'll have to pay for that computer he just threw out the window."

"Pinky swear doesn't cut it anymore. My attorney has a few documents for you to sign."

"I looked over your resume, and the good news is I like the paper it's typed on. Do you really want to know the bad news?"

"Your resume states that you've worked with 2 presidents, won the Nobel Prize and climbed Mt. Everest. That's all fine and dandy, but how are you at telemarketing?"

"I don't know which is harder-- getting Smythe started in the morning, or his computer."

"I'm sorry, but I can't hire you. I typed your name in on a search engine, and lazy, selfish and unmotivated were the categories that came up."

"You had enough power in our cell phone to make one last call, and instead of getting us rescued, you cancel your tee-time?"

"The boss thinks you've been slacking. So, he wants to keep an eye on you."

"*Good news, Franklin! I figured out how to cut costs, and raise office morale. You're fired.*"

The End.

To further support this author, kindly post a review after you finish this book

Join Newsletter list
To join Bianca Ku's Newsletter and be notified about FREE book promos and when new books are released by the author,
Click here to join Bianca Ku's Newsletter list

For more books by this author, visit
Amazon's Bianca Ku's Page
Books
Turkey Farts
Dog Farts
Santa Farts
Fart Diary

Made in the USA
Middletown, DE
31 July 2015